JESSE
HUNTER

YOU
MEAN
THE WORLD
TO ME

hardie grant books
MELBOURNE · LONDON

Published in 2015 by Hardie Grant Books

Hardie Grant Books (Australia)
Ground Floor, Building 1
658 Church Street
Richmond, Victoria 3121
www.hardiegrant.com.au

Hardie Grant Books (UK)
5th & 6th Floor
52-54 Southwark Street
London SE1 1RU
www.hardiegrant.co.uk

Cataloguing-in-Publication data is available from the National Library of Australia.

You Mean the World to Me
ISBN: 9781742709956

Concept, design and photography: Jesse Hunter
Design liaison: Mikala Robinson-Koss

www.alltheloveintheworld.co
@jessehunter_author (Instagram)
facebook.com/alltheloveintheworldthebook

Colour reproduction by Splitting Image Colour Studio
Printed in China by 1010 Printing International Limited

YOU MEAN THE WORLD TO ME

JESSE HUNTER

7 THE JOURNEY

9 MY WORLD

10 YOU MEAN THE WORLD TO ME

157 ABUNDANT THANKS

159 OTHER BOOKS BY JESSE HUNTER

160 AUTHOR QUOTE

THE JOURNEY

I HAVE TRAVELLED THROUGH 49 COUNTRIES
IN MY 33 YEARS ON THIS BEAUTIFUL PLANET OF OURS
AND DISCOVERED THAT EVERY SINGLE HUMAN BEING
JUST WANTS TO BE LOVED.

NO MATTER YOUR RACE, SEX, AGE, RELIGION
OR SOCIAL STATUS YOU MEAN THE WORLD TO SOMEONE
AND SOMEONE MEANS THE WORLD TO YOU.

For my Loves
Mikaela and Indi

9

I could watch sunsets with you forever

Gotland SWEDEN 13

WE'LL GO PLACES

YOU NEVER DREAMED EXISTED

Santorini, GREECE 21

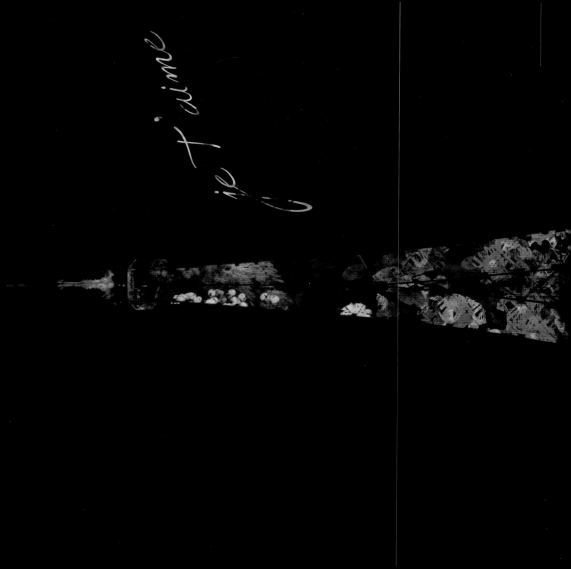

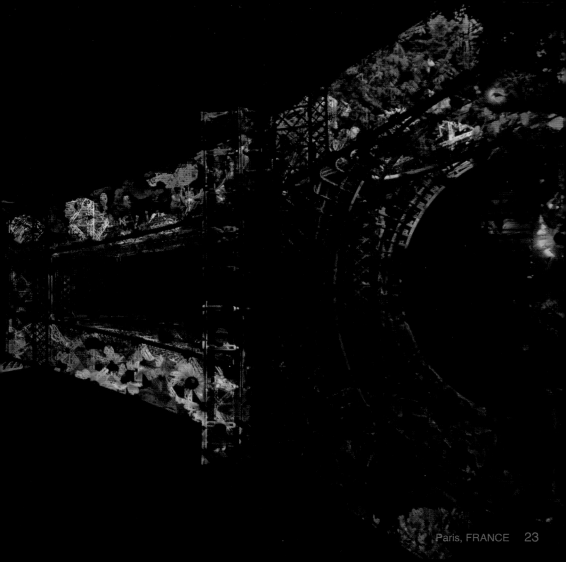

EVERY

SET

SHINE

BRIGHT

LIKE A

DIAMOND

The Serengeti, TANZANIA

I'd walk a thousand miles for you

You stand
out from the crowd

BE
FREE

Inie Lake, BURMA 43

Sihanoukville CAMBODIA 49

DREAMING OF AN ENDLESS SUMMER WITH YOU

58 Cusco, PERU

60 Berlin, GERMANY

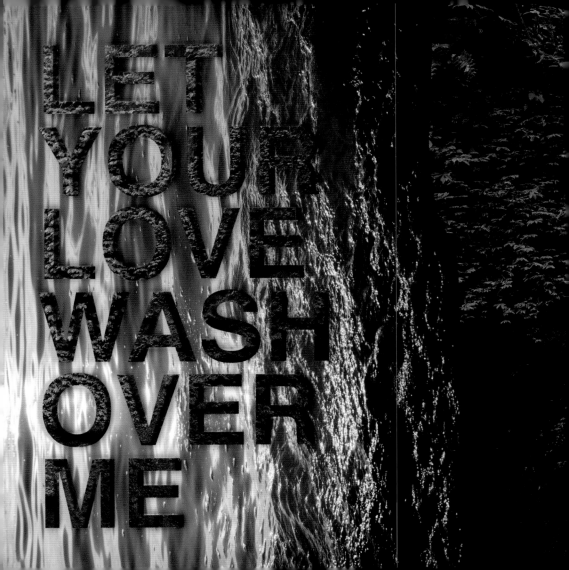

Let the light in

Be your own kind o

BEAUTIFUL

Valparaíso, CHILE 73

YESTERDAY IS HISTORY

TOMORROW IS A MYSTERY

TODAY IS A GIFT

THAT'S WHY IT'S CALLED THE PRESENT

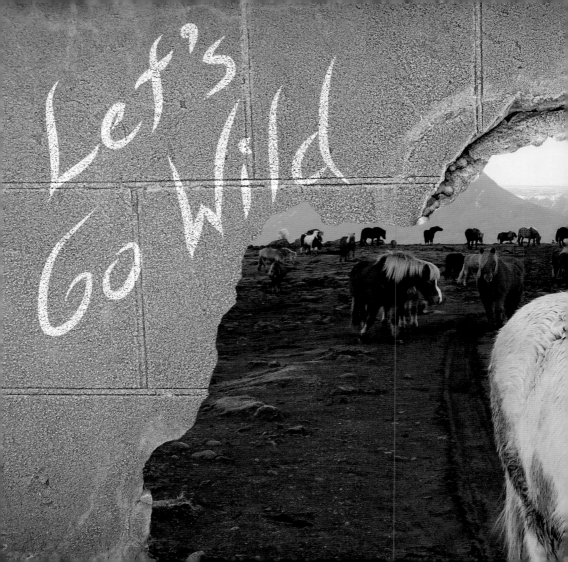

DOMUS BALTHASAR

the map to my heart is yours

Let's explore the world

TOGETHER

Nature will show us the way.

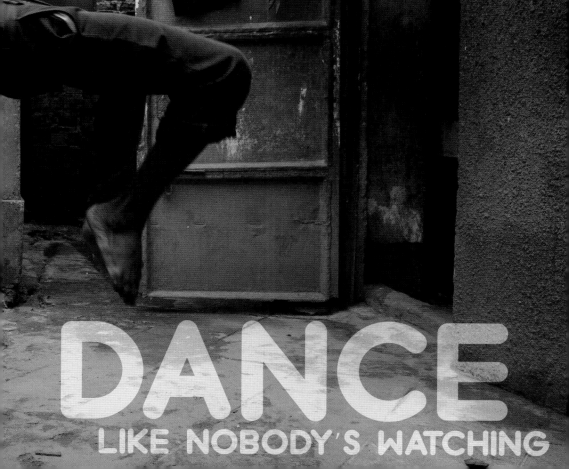

Sunsets
were
made
for
us

YOU ARE PUURFECT

I ♥ HANGING OUT WITH U

Leap for your dreams......

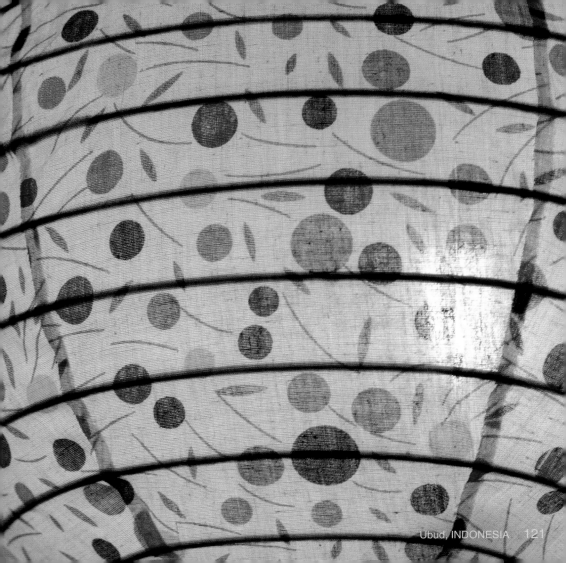

Ubud, INDONESIA 121

Just Breathe

THANK YOU FOR

ALWAYS

LISTENING TO ME

FROM DAWN

I'LL BE THINKING

UNTIL DUSK

ABOUT YOU

THANK YOU MIKALA AND INDI FOR INSPIRING ME MOMENT BY MOMENT, DAY BY DAY. THANK YOU MUM AND DAD FOR YOUR CONSTANT LOVE, GENEROSITY AND SUPPORT. TO ALL MY FAMILY AND FRIENDS WHO CONTINUALLY SUPPORT MY WORK I THANK YOU. SPECIAL THANKS TO MY FAMILY AND FRIENDS WHO FED OR HOUSED MIKALA AND I DURING OUR JOURNEY AROUND THE WORLD. YOU ALL TRULY MEAN THE WORLD TO ME.

THANK YOU

JESSE HUNTER

@jessehunter_author

facebook.com/alltheloveintheworldthebook

@jessehunterauth

OTHER BOOKS BY JESSE HUNTER

@alltheloveintheworldthebook

facebook.com/alltheloveintheworldthebook

@allthehappinessintheworld

facebook.com/allthehappinessintheworldthebook

@allthecatsintheworldthebook

facebook.com/allthecatsintheworldthebook

Always know that you mean the world to someone.

- Jesse Hunter